Will Monday Ever Come?

Sheila M. Blackburn

The third book in Set A of
Sam's Football Stories

Dedication
For My Mum.
With thanks to Tom for all the support
and understanding.

Ackowledgements
With thanks to *The Boots Company* and *Delmar Press in Nantwich*,
for their support of this project.

Published by Brilliant Publications
1 Church View
Sparrow Hall Farm
Edlesborough
Dunstable
Beds LU6 2ES

Telephone: 01525 229720
Fax: 01525 229725
e-mail: sales@brilliantpublications.co.uk
website: www.brilliantpublications.co.uk

Written by Sheila M. Blackburn
Illustrated by Tony O'Donnell of Graham Cameron Illustration

© Sheila M. Blackburn 2002

ISBN 1 903853 192 Set A – 6 titles: Football Crazy, Team Talk, Will Monday Ever Come?, Training Night, If Only Dad Could See Us! and A Place on the Team.
ISBN 1 903853 036 Set B – 6 titles: The First Match, Trouble for Foz, What about the Girls?, What's Worrying Eddie?, Nowhere to Train and Are We the Champions?

Printed in England by Ashford Colour Press Ltd
First published in 2002
10 9 8 7 6 5 4 3 2 1

The right of Sheila Blackburn to be identified as the author of this work have been asserted by her in accordance with the Copyright, Designs and Patents Act 1988.

Sam's Football Stories

After the football meeting at his house, Sam had to wait a whole week for the first training.

Sam was not very good at waiting.

Every morning, he made a mark
on the football calendar in his bedroom.

He counted the days and he put
a big circle round the next Monday.

The week went very slowly and
things did not go well for Sam.

Will Monday Ever Come?

In school on Tuesday, he just had to chat to Danny about the meeting the night before.

Miss Hill got so cross that she gave them both extra work at break time.

Sam and Danny missed playing football with the others.

Danny wasn't allowed to eat his snack. He was really mad.

He said he needed food so that he'd be strong for football.

Sam's Football Stories

After break time, they tried to be good.

"I'm not going to talk to you again," said Sam.
So Sam kept quiet for the rest of the morning.

It was different after playing football at lunch-time.
The two boys couldn't stop talking.

Miss Hill was even more cross.
"Very well, you two," she said.
"I have made up my mind.
You will have to sit away from each other."

"Oh, Miss! That's not fair!" said Danny.

He liked to sit with Sam so that he could
ask him how to do the work.

"Then you can choose, if you like," said Miss Hill.
"Either you sit apart for a few days, or
you can miss outdoor games this week."

Miss football?

That did it!

Sam and Danny chose to not sit together
for the rest of the week.

Will Monday Ever Come?

On Wednesday, Danny came to Sam's house after
school.

They had a big tea and Danny had
seconds of everything.

Then they went up to Sam's room.
At first, they looked at football books and pictures.
They were quiet.

Then they got out a foam ball.

Sam did some headers and Danny was goalie.

The goal was the end of Sam's bed.
It was great fun, but it got very noisy.
In the end, Danny did a dive and missed.
He bounced off the bed and landed on the floor.

Thump!

Mum came running upstairs.
"What on earth is going on?" she shouted.

She saw Danny on the floor.

Sam tried not to laugh, but Danny looked funny.

"You are not to play football in the house!"
said Mum. "It's not funny, Sam. Stop laughing!"

Sam tried but couldn't help himself.

Danny had to go home.

Sam was sent to bed early.

Thursday and Friday were cold, wet days.

Outdoor games was off because of the rain.

Some of the children said good,
because it was too cold to go outside.

Most of the class said it was not fair.
Sam and Danny did a lot of moaning.

In the end, Miss Hill said they could do games in the school hall.

"Can we do football with a soft ball?" asked Sam.

Some of the class groaned.

"No," said Miss Hill. "Let's play something
that everyone likes."

"Not fair!" said Danny to Sam.

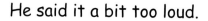

He said it a bit too loud.

Miss Hill heard him.
"Shall we stay in class and work?" she said.

"No, sorry, Miss!"

They played team games in the hall.

Sam's Football Stories

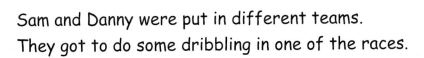

Sam and Danny were put in different teams.
They got to do some dribbling in one of the races.

On Saturday, Sam and Danny met at the wasteland.

"I can't stay long," said Danny.
"I have to go and see my grandad.
It's his birthday."

Sam was sorry, but not too sad.
He knew Danny really liked his grandad.
He wouldn't want to miss his birthday.

They kicked the ball about for a bit.

After all the rain, the wasteland was very muddy.

"Mum said not to get dirty," said Danny.
They looked at his jeans and trainers.
They were covered in spots of mud.

"Oh dear!" said Sam.
"I'll get done," said Danny.
"I'd better go."

"See you on Monday."

Sam took the ball home.
He did a bit of dribbling.
He dodged round the gate.
He didn't mean to kick the ball hard.

Crash!

The shed window smashed and
the ball flew inside. It hit some tins of paint and
they fell off the shelf.

Sam's Football Stories

It was funny how his dad came out so quickly.

"Sorry, Dad!" said Sam.

"Go inside!" shouted Dad.
He kept the ball.

Sam was grounded for the rest of the weekend.

Sam's Football Stories

Sam went to bed early on Saturday night.
He read his football books for a bit
and he looked at all his stickers.

"Just a few more to go," he said to himself,
"then I'll have the whole set."

Mum came up with milk for his supper.
She had made some cookies too.

"Is Dad still mad?" Sam wanted to know.

"A bit," said Mum. "He's still mending the shed
window."

Sam drank his milk and ate two cookies.

"Will he let me out tomorrow?"

"I don't think so," said Mum.
"You've been grounded for the rest of the weekend."

"That's ages!" said Sam. "What will I do
all day?"

"Something will come up," said Mum. "You'll see.
Now come on. Time to clean your teeth."

Early on Sunday morning, Sam got up and crept downstairs.

He closed the kitchen door behind him
and began to make breakfast.

He had done it a few times before,
so he knew what to do.

Just as the kettle was boiling, Mum came down.

"Hello, Sam. What's all this?"

Sam looked at his feet.

"Sorry about the shed window," he said.

"Is this your way of making up?"

Sam nodded. Mum knew him so well.

"You need to say sorry to your dad really, Sam.
He was the one who had to mend the window."

"Dad always works on Saturdays," said Sam.
"Why was he here yesterday?"

"He got home early," said Mum.
"He was going to watch some sport on TV."

Sam felt really bad.

Mum looked at the pot of tea he had made.
"Take him a cup of tea and
tell him you're sorry," she said.

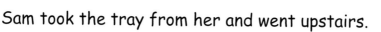

Sam took the tray from her and went upstairs.

Dad sat up in bed and looked at him.
"Hello, Sam," he said.

Perhaps he wasn't as cross this morning.
Sam put the tray down by the bed and looked at Dad.

"Sorry about the window, Dad.
Sorry I messed up your afternoon."

Dad sipped his tea.
"This is good," he said. "Did you make it?"

Sam nodded.
"I wanted to say sorry."

"How would you like to help me today?" Dad asked.

"Aren't you going to work today, Dad?"

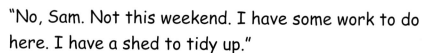

"No, Sam. Not this weekend. I have some work to do here. I have a shed to tidy up."

"I'd like to help," said Sam.

He was glad to have something to do.

They started after breakfast.

Sam's Football Stories

First, they cleaned up after the spilled paint.
Then Dad said they might as well
clear out the whole shed.

There was a lot of rubbish, so they took it to the tip.

Sam went on and on about the football team
and Eddie Ford and the training.

Dad smiled.
He had been like this when he was a boy.

Later on when all the work was finished,
Dad got the football out.
He had put it in a secret hiding place.

They did some passing and shooting.

Dad set up the goal posts.

"I enjoyed that," said Dad at teatime.
"Yeah! It was great," said Sam.

Sam's Football Stories

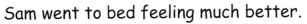

Sam went to bed feeling much better.
Dad wasn't cross any more.
"Besides, tomorrow is Monday!" Sam said to himself.
"Our first training night!"

Sam lay looking up at his United poster.

"It's hard sometimes when you're training
to be a footballer," Sam said to himself, and
he fell asleep.

We hope that you enjoyed this book. To find out what happens next, look for the next book in the series.

Set A

Football Crazy

Team Talk

Will Monday Ever Come?

Training Night

If Only Dad Could See Us!

A Place on the Team

Set B

The First Match

Trouble for Foz

What about the Girls?

What's Worrying Eddie?

Nowhere to Train

Are We the Champions?